Devon r
that time forgot

a driver's guide to ancient highways

Paul White

Bossiney Books • Launceston

First published 2006 by
Bossiney Books Ltd, Langore, Launceston, Cornwall PL15 8LD
www.bossineybooks.com
ISBN 0-1-899383-87-5
ISBN 978-189938387-0

Acknowledgements
The map on page 2 is by Graham Hallowell,
those on pages 6, 12 and 18 by John Ogilby
Printed in Great Britain by St Austell Printing Company

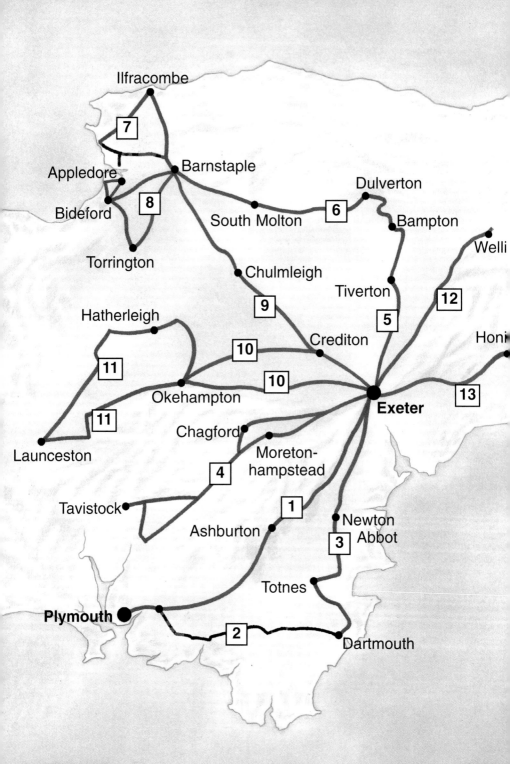

Introduction

This book is an introduction to a bizarre activity – 'Ogilby-roading'.

The aim is to follow, as closely as is possible, the ancient main roads of Devon. These were mapped for the first time in 1675 by John Ogilby, when there were no wheeled vehicles in the South-West. The majority still exist as narrow lanes, whilst others remain as lesser rights of way – as footpaths, bridleways and other by-ways. Some of these minor rights of way need better legal protection from 'off-roaders' who damage their surfaces and spoil the enjoyment of other people. This book is intended for motorists who are prepared to respect history and the landscape, and keep to the tarmac which already covers so much of the country.

Why bother to identify and follow the old roads? Some people enjoy the detective work and the comparison of old maps with modern ones. Those with a romantic sense of the past can imagine medieval monks or Stuart post-boys riding the lanes – and it is certain that some great names in our history travelled by these routes, Drake and Ralegh, Cromwell and John Wesley. But the main point of following the drives in this book is for the delightful places you will find – places which once were 'on the beaten track' when that is literally what the highways were, but which have been 'out of the way' for a couple of centuries or more. In some of these places it is very hard to believe that the 21st century exists.

Devon 'roads' in 1675 were no better than muddy bridleways through hill country: contemporary writers described Devon as 'mountainous' (their experience of mountains was limited) but when riding in a car on a well-engineered road, it is easy to be unaware how hilly Devon actually is.

There were until after 1750 quite literally no wheeled vehicles in use west of Exeter. The roads had developed over four thousand years for people on foot or horseback and for trains of pack animals. These ancient tracks went in relatively direct lines from A to B – we had straight highways long before the Romans came – and took really steep hills in their stride. Where their route was not direct, it was to avoid boggy ground, or to hug a ridge. Typically they ran along ridges, descending into the valleys only to cross a river, then climbing as quickly as possible to the top of the hill on the other side. One particularly fine example can still be walked: it runs south from Grimspound on Dartmoor, passing numerous prehistoric burial mounds positioned beside it along the ridge. Our roads didn't change a lot from prehistoric times until the late 18th century.

From about 1750 to about 1840 the road network was upgraded to carry wheeled traffic. The financial mechanism for this was the turnpike trust system, under which tolls were charged by a private company and the proceeds used to maintain the road. The 'turnpike' was originally a simple form of gate, but the roads themselves soon came to be called 'turnpikes'.

Then, quite abruptly, the road system was all but abandoned for three generations following a technological breakthrough – railways.

In Devon and Cornwall, though probably not in most parts of England, it is still possible to drive many of the ancient roads today because of their particular history. In the early phases of the road improvements – from 1750 to around 1815 – the existing tracks were given a poor quality gravel surface and their hedges were kept trimmed. A few were widened just sufficiently for a carriage to pass, but even then most remained single-track. In other respects they were left largely untouched.

In the later phase of road improvement (1815-1840), following advances in civil engineering techniques, most of Devon's ancient roads as mapped by John Ogilby were found inadequate for use as highways, mainly because of their steep gradients. They were replaced by totally new roads using routes such as river valleys which the old roads had avoided. It was a massive investment in infrastructure which within just a few years appeared to have been a total waste of resources; the railways took over.

In the 20th century, as roads came back into use due to widening car ownership, those roads which had been turnpiked in the early phase, along with a wide network of other minor roads, were given tarmacadam surfaces; they include perhaps 80% of the roads Ogilby mapped in 1675.

In flatter parts of England (and surprisingly even in East Devon, much of which is far from flat) many Ogilby routes were found acceptable. The width and the road surface were progressively improved. Some dual carriageways are actually Ogilby routes, but their original character has totally disappeared – they are functional but not fun to drive.

4

Driving Ogilby's roads

This is by no means a book of easy drives. These are roads which have remained little changed, apart from a tarmac surface, since they were condemned as utterly inadequate for horse traffic 200 years ago, so you should not expect them to meet today's standards!

They are almost all narrow: few of them justify white lines down the centre. Sometimes they are just wide enough for two cars to pass with care, sometimes they are of inconsistent width, sometimes single track with passing places. And just a few are a unique Devonian contribution to motoring – the single track road without passing places. At one point (not included in this book) I once had to reverse half a mile…

Where there are really difficult sections, I have given alternative routes. In these cases, in 'Route A', the A is for Authentic – the Ogilby route – and Route B is 'Better'. They rejoin at the ☞ sign.

Those of us who drive many miles on Devon lanes get used to them, and either acquire adequate driving techniques or in a few cases both four-wheel-drives and aggressive attitudes. Rural driving should be a cooperative venture rather than a competition. If we can give and receive favours, and always acknowledge each other, it can be quite a civilised experience! But even if we all behave perfectly, narrow roads and single track roads alike require sustained concentration. If you are unused to them, you may find the experience exhausting, so don't do too much of it in one day.

There are some golden rules for single track driving. The first, of course, is never be in a hurry. You need to be able to stop in less than half the distance you can see, since the other driver may be going too fast. If this means slow walking pace round a corner, so be it. You may need to use the horn at blind bends. On the worst stretches, try to keep a window partly open so that you can hear oncoming traffic and, as a bonus, the birds.

Passing places are usually adequate for just one car. Don't get too close to the car in front: if a bunch of cars going one way meets more than one car going the other way, the result can be gridlock. If someone behind you wants to go faster, pull in to a passing place and allow them to overtake.

Sooner or later you will encounter walkers, or a horse and rider.

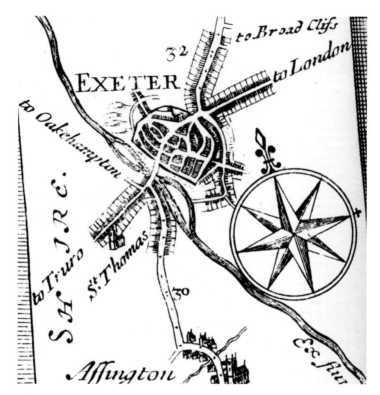

Remember it is your new-fangled horseless carriage which is out of place here, not them! Horses can easily be 'spooked' by meeting a car, as also can mothers with push-chairs. Stop for horses and allow them to pass by you. In very narrow lanes, do the same for walkers; even when you are overtaking them, it is far safer to ask them to walk back past you, rather than risk crushing their feet as you force your way past.

Cycling

Many of the routes may well be suitable for cycling, which would be much more environmentally friendly than driving. Not being a cyclist myself, I have not attempted to assess the routes for this purpose.

Maps

I assume that as a basic minimum you will have a UK road atlas, so that you cannot get irretrievably lost in the lanes. If you have the relevant Ordnance Survey maps, however, whether the 1:50,000 or 1:25,000, you will be able to understand the route better.

The routes

1 Exeter to Plympton

Distance: 37 miles
Approximate time: 1 1/2 hours
Character: At least as far as Ivybridge, this is a most attractive route, through lovely woodland over Haldon, and then unexpectedly tranquil countryside with several interesting towns and attractive villages.

Start from the Sainsbury superstore on the Alphington Road. Turn left out of the car park, then immediately left (ALPHINGTON/DAWLISH) but after 500 yards keep right (ALPHINGTON) to pass Alphington church, then turn right at a double roundabout (SHILLINGFORD ST GEORGE).

Drive through both Shillingfords and descend a steep hill into Clapham, where our road turns abruptly left. Bear right (UNDERDOWN) and head steadily uphill. At two crossroads continue ahead (CHUDLEIGH), then descend steadily through attractive woodland. Cross over the A38 and enter Chudleigh. Turn right at the war memorial.

Chudleigh is an old town but was destroyed by a fire in 1807, so there are few buildings older than that. At the end of the town, cross A38 again, keep left and after 800 yards turn right (CH. KNIGHTON/BOVEY TRACEY). Within Chudleigh Knighton, keep left, then right at a mini-roundabout, before following signs to join the A38 westbound (PLYMOUTH).

(The old road actually kept right within Chudleigh Knighton, traversed Knighton Heath to the north of the clay pit and, by what is now a bridle-way, crossed the Teign and passed in front of Heathfield Primary School.)

Alphington's most famous inhabitant was probably 'Mr Micawber'. Charles Dickens personified his feckless father John as Mr Micawber in *David Copperfield*, and it was here in Alphington at Mile End Cottage (on the right 100 yards beyond Mill Lane) that he relocated his parents – at a considerable distance from his own home in Kent and from John Dickens's London creditors. 'Mr Micawber' started forging cheques in his son's name, so the move did not solve the problem…

Leave the A38 very soon, signed A382, and take the third exit (ILSING-TON) which soon reveals itself as the former A38 – one of those deadly roads which were common when I was a child, with an overtaking lane in the middle to be used by traffic in both directions!

After just over a mile, cross over the dual carriageway. Some 800 yards past the Welcome Stranger pub, turn left onto a minor road (unmarked, and on a bend) up what is a still older line of the Exeter-Plymouth road. This single track lane leads up to the old centre of Bickington.

Keep left (NEWTON ABBOT) and in a few yards go straight ahead, rather than following the 'main' road to the left. Drive on down to cross a stream (the River Lemon) and up to the A383. You will get a good view of the substantial engineering which went into building the turnpike in 1819. Turn right on A383 (ASHBURTON), noticing the tall Georgian building on your right, which reveals its origin by its name – the Traveller's Rest. Then join the A38 again in the Plymouth direction.

Leave the A38 at the ASHBURTON turn and cross the dual carriageway to drive through this attractive and interesting old town. Follow the old main road as it runs almost straight through the town to a T-junction, with a petrol station ahead of you.

Turn left and almost immediately right (BUCKFAST/BUCKFASTLEIGH). After 1½ miles at a T-junction turn right, then keep left at the mini-roundabout, to skirt Buckfastleigh. The old road would of course have passed through this little town, which is well worth a detour to explore; it seems to have turned its back on tourism, despite the presence on its doorstep of two major attractions, Buckfast Abbey itself and the South Devon Railway.

Dean Prior was home to the 17th century poet, Robert Herrick, who produced a stream of cheerful rustic poems while he was vicar of the church here – though by nature he was urbane, and privately he felt desperately isolated in such a rural setting. He seems to have formed a long-lasting relationship with his housekeeper Prudence Baldwin, who is remembered by a memorial in the church of Dean Prior.

Continue along B3380 as far as you can, then turn right and enter the village of Upper Dean.

Within the village, bear right (DEANCOMBE), then immediately left (unsigned) up the old village street. After 200 yards, the present lane turns sharp left: the ancient road went straight on, and it can still be seen as a holloway, worn into a trough by centuries of use, and climbing steeply.

At a junction, turn right (HARBOURNEFORD) and after 0.7 miles you'll find the ancient road rejoining the modern lane in the form of a track from the right. Continue through Harbourneford, noticing the old foot-bridge to the left as you cross a stream, and onward to South Brent.

At a T-junction, keep left along Fore Steet, then right, and head down towards the river. Turn right onto a major road, then very soon turn right again (BRENT MILL). Cross the bridge, keep right for GLAZEBROOK, then follow signs towards CHESTON, then to SHUTE CROSS and WRANGATON.

At Wrangaton, a Saxon cross to the left of the road suggests the antiquity of this route. It lasted till 1819, when what is now the B3213 was built parallel to it, itself now superseded by the dual carriageway. There is a steep and tricky descent at Bittaford, then we turn right onto B3213. Before the railway viaduct was built, this ancient road may have descended even more precipitously to the old bridge, which lies just to the north of the viaduct. Ogilby's map shows no settlement at all here in 1675.

We now follow B3213 into Ivybridge – where once again there seems to have been no settlement in 1675. At a mini-roundabout, go forward and drive (slowly!) down Fore Street. Go forward at a roundabout, and join the A38 towards PLYMOUTH.

After 4 miles take the exit for B3416 PLYMPTON and at the T-junction turn right (PLYMPTON). At a roundabout, turn left (B3416 PLYMPTON) onto Ridgeway. This is both the name of a road, and also the name of the central shopping area of modern Plympton.

The main road into south Cornwall in 1675 passed through Ridgeway, followed the Plymouth Road to Marsh Mills, then Laira Road to Lipson Vale and Lipson Road to the present city centre, continuing down Millbay Road to Stonehouse and the Cremyll Ferry. Whilst this route can be fol-lowed, little historical atmosphere remains: so I suggest instead exploring an extraordinary survival, the medieval borough town of Plympton St Maurice, also known as Plympton Earl, with its Norman castle and attractive Fore Street.

Presumably in medieval times the main road passed this way, but by 1675 it avoided the decaying borough. WG Hoskins, writing in 1954, said 'one smells cow-dung in the streets instead of petrol fumes: the immemorial life-giving smell of the land from which the little town took its birth in the 12th century'. You are more likely to smell fresh paint than cow dung these days, as such gems no longer go unnoticed.

Take the second left, New Park Road, which leads into Longcause, and park somewhere near the church, to explore on foot.

2 Plymouth to Dartmouth

Approximate distance: 28 miles
Approximate time: 1 1/2 hours
Character: Attractive South Hams countryside. Between Plympton and Yealmbridge the route is in places very narrow – but this is easily avoided by joining the A379 further west, at Plymouth, Brixton or Yealmpton. Then there's an easy section to Modbury, and a fairly good route all the way to Dartmouth – unless you choose to follow the true ancient route through Brownston, which is very narrow indeed with few passing places.

Start from the Sainsbury's superstore beside the A38 at Marsh Mills. Leaving the car park at the exit beside the flyover, take the third exit at the roundabout (B3417 PLYMPTON). Follow this to the next roundabout, where you have a choice.

To explore Plympton
The most interesting part of Plympton is Plympton St Maurice, with its Norman castle and old town main street, so if you don't already know it, it is worth a diversion (see previous route). Take the second exit at the mini-roundabout and immediately turn right into Market Road. Turn left at the T-junction with Underwood Road. Follow the major lane, and keep right into Fore Street. You may well want to park and explore this medieval borough and its Norman castle on foot.

At the far end of Fore Street, when it bears off to the right, turn left up Longbrook Street/George Lane. Pass the church and turn right at the crossroads into Longcause. This will lead you, by way (briefly) of Waggon Hill and then of New Park Road, out to Ridgeway, which was Ogilby's actual route through Plympton. Turn right and continue to a roundabout. Skip the next paragraph.

Alternatively, take the second exit at the roundabout, which is Ridgeway – the ancient main road, which ran straight through the heart of the town; now traffic is diverted to the south of the shopping street. Go forward at the mini-roundabout and continue to the next roundabout.

☞ Turn right (EXETER A38) but cross the dual carriageway, ignoring the turns both for Exeter and Plymouth. Then take the very first left, which is unsigned. After 200 yards, turn right – but notice the track joining from the left, which is a good example of how a major highway might have looked in 1675, though perhaps without the fly-tipping.

Descend through a gorge – one of the deepest holloways I know. No wonder this route was known as Deep Lane. After about 250 yards, go forward at a junction, joining a slightly wider lane.

At Efford Farm, cross a stream and keep left (YEALMPTON). At a staggered crossroads, forward (YEO PARK). Pass a housing estate and go forward at another crossroads. On reaching A379, turn left and cross the Yealm. As the tollhouse reminds you, you have now joined the turnpike road: the rate board is still in position. A shilling was the toll for a carriage and horses to cover a few miles: at that time farm workers were paid no more than eight shillings for a six day week.

After 2.3 miles keep right (A379) to cross two branches of the Erme. You now have a choice.

Route B (the better route)
Follow A379 into Modbury.

Route A (the authentic route)
Take the first on the right after crossing the Erme towards ORCHETON, then turn first left, soon joining another lane. (After a further 300 yards, a foot-path on the right signed RUNAWAY LANE is the ancient highway.) This lane

brings you back to A379 where you turn right, bringing you into Modbury.

☞ At the main crossroads at the centre of Modbury, just beyond the Exeter Inn, turn left (DARTMOUTH) up Brownston Street. Some 1.5 miles from the edge of Modbury, the B3207 bears right whilst an unmarked lane goes straight ahead, to Brownston.

Route B (the very much better route)
Follow the B3207, which swings well to the right of Brownston, briefly joins the B3196, then turns right at California Cross (MORELEIGH/DARTMOUTH).

Route A (the authentic route)
The ancient road is the unmarked lane through Brownston. It is *very narrow indeed*, with few passing places – the kind of lane where, if you meet walkers, you should stop and allow them to squeeze past you rather than driving past them. Turn right at Brownston Forge. If you go this way, you will arrive at California Cross and go straight over for MORELEIGH/HALWELL/DARTMOUTH.

☞ The next feature is Gara Bridge, a most attractive spot. Continue on through the village of Moreleigh. At a junction, you will be directed right for DARTMOUTH, and you may wish to follow the signs, but a short stretch of single track road with passing places will take you there much more directly. Turn left (HALWELL), descending then briefly climbing.

Turn left on A381, then just before the church turn right on A3122 for DARTMOUTH. The main road follows the old line quite closely, except for the actual descent into the town.

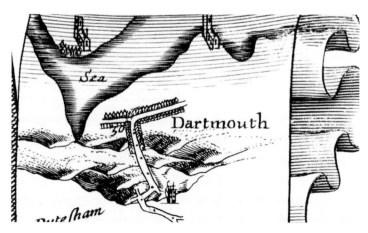

3 Dartmouth to Exeter

Distance: 36 miles
Approximate time: 2 hours (plus time in the ferry queue)
Character: Despite passing through a densely populated part of Devon, this route is largely rural, running through extremely pretty countryside dotted with picture postcard cob and thatch cottages – not to mention a couple of castles. For much of the way it uses very narrow lanes.

In 1675 this was part of a longer route, from Dartmouth to Minehead, which Ogilby describes as '…affording in general no very good way, as being exceeding hilly, but everywhere replenished with inns etc for entertaining and accommodating travellers; a well frequented road, as being the ready way from Dartmouth a port town on the South Sea to the city of Exeter, and thence to Minehead a port town on the North Sea.'

We start by taking the Lower Ferry across to Kingswear, then follow B3205 until it meets A379 at Hillhead, where we turn right (PAIGNTON) then take the first exit at the roundabout.

Rather surprisingly, the A380, which you might assume to be a 1930s bypass for Paignton, is in fact the ancient highway.

Route A (the authentic and easy but rather boring route!)
If you really want to follow the Ogilby route, then you take the A380 as far as Marldon, where you bear left into the village at the first roundabout, carry on past the post office and primary school, both on the left, keep right (COMPTON) down Village Road, and perhaps stop and wait for the rest of us at the Church House pub. Skip the next five paragraphs and we'll join you there.

Route B (on other old roads, with some narrow sections)
I propose a more interesting diversion, following ancient roads which Ogilby himself did not map, but which existed in his time. Heading towards Paignton, you will meet a major road, the A3022 from Brixham. Turn left, signed A379.

Within 400 yards of that junction, you will cross the Paignton & Dartmouth Steam Railway at Churston Station. Immediately after the railway bridge, turn left into Greenway Road.

At a junction, keep left, then at the Manor Inn bear right for WADDETON and STOKE GABRIEL. Cross the Paignton-Stoke Gabriel road and follow signs for AISH and then for TOTNES.

When William of Orange came to England by invitation to oust James II in 1688, he landed with his small army at Brixham. The army started heading inland by the 'Ogilby route' – I'm sure William's supporters had given his staff copies of Ogilby's road atlas. One can only attempt to imagine what taking an army along one of these 'roads' was like, especially if they had artillery with them! William himself sensibly kept out of the way of his army, and took the alternative route we are following. He held a council of war at Parliament House, which you will pass on your left.

Continue to the junction with A385, the Totnes to Paignton road, turn left then immediately right (BERRY POMEROY). Turn right at the centre of the village (next to, but not at, a mini-roundabout).

Berry Pomeroy Castle is clearly signed off to the left, and you may well want to visit it, then return to this spot. Turn left at the mini-roundabout in Marldon, passing the post office and the school, then keep right (COMPTON) down Village Road, and pass the Church House pub.

Church houses were common in Devon; many people had to walk a distance to get to church, and the church house provided refreshments (including home-brewed ale) and a resting place for them. It was both the village hall and a natural social centre, and over the centuries it metamorphosed gently into the village pub.

☞ Pass the pub on your left, and continue down Love Lane. Turn left at a T-junction and follow the road through Compton, then past Compton Castle on your left. Take the first on the right (NORTH WHILBOROUGH) then first left (STONEYCOMBE) and follow signs to ABBOTSKERSWELL.

At Maddacombe Cross and again at Greatoak Cross, go straight ahead (unsigned). This really is a lost road – it should be signed as 'Yᵉ highway to Exeter & London' but now it doesn't even merit a fingerpost to get us to Abbotskerswell!

Turn right at Abbotskerswell Post Office and after 200 yards bear left up

STONEMANS HILL which leads you towards Newton Abbot. The ancient route used what are now footpaths to cut across the fields to Wolborough Church, then down to Newton Abbot, but you will have to follow the tarmac. On reaching the cemetery gate, however, you can turn right, then as the road veers round to the right, turn really sharp left down Old Totnes Road (which is old but not ancient!), bear right, then join the modern Totnes road into Newton Abbot.

Keep left at two roundabouts, following signs for A382 BOVEY TRACEY. Go forward at traffic lights, then right at the next roundabout and take the first exit at the fourth roundabout. After 500 yards, bear right down a minor road (TEIGNGRACE). This is Old Exeter Road. Cross a long causeway and several bridges and go forward at a roundabout: this straight stretch is the line of a major Roman road – a rarity in Devon. You now have a choice.

I have not been able to trace for certain the exact route of the 17th century road over Haldon, if indeed there was a single route: quite often there were multiple paths over such uncultivated areas. More than one subsequent route, now abandoned, has left traces in the landscape.

Whatever route was taken has been overlaid by forestry plantations and just possibly also by the landscaping of Ugbrooke Park. I suspect the ancient route approximated to the dual carriageway as far as Wapperwell, then took a more or less direct route to Beggars Bush.

The choice is between a dual carriageway across the Haldon Hills, or an attractive few miles of rather narrow single-track lane through wooded farmland before joining the A380.

For the dual carriageway, follow the road round to the right and pick up signs for EXETER A380.

For the woodland road, continue straight ahead on the line of the Roman road (SANDYGATE/GAPPAH) instead of bearing off to the right. Pass the Sandygate Inn. In 1675 you would soon have passed a second pub with the unusual name of Tom the Trumpeter.

Continue until the Roman road becomes a track and you are forced to the left. Keep right at the first junction (BABCOMBE), and after 0.7 miles at a T-junction turn left. Pass through the hamlet of Gappah and follow the main lane as it turns right. Ignore a left turn. On your right you will see a long tall wall which defines the Ugbrooke estate, then you will pass the town of Chudleigh downhill to your left.

Go forward at a tricky junction (EXETER). Ignore side turnings. In due course you will be back to the probable line of the ancient road, which descends past Waddon Brakes and rejoins A380.

☞ For a final flurry of intermittent authenticity, follow the signs into and through KENNFORD, then at the far end of the village, cross the bridge over the dual carriageway, turn right and join A379. Immediately after crossing over the A30, take the left turn to ALPHINGTON.

4 A Dartmoor circuit – Exeter, Tavistock and back

Distance: 62 miles
Approximate time: 2¹/₂ hours
Character: This drive follows the 17th century post-road to Chagford and as far as possible traces its route as it crossed the Moor. The Dartmoor scenery is of course stunning, and the off-moor sections are very pretty. One stretch, the seven miles from Dunsford towards Chagford, is very narrow, with few passing places. From personal experience, may I suggest you avoid the 'school run' time! If you prefer to omit the narrowest part, this is easily done by continuing on the main road from Dunsford to Moretonhampstead, then turning right onto A382 and left when signed into Chagford. The equally attractive return journey is by 'normal' roads.

From the Exe Bridges, take B3212 (MORETONHAMPSTEAD) through the early suburb of St Thomas. After a mile, it ducks under the A30, signed MORETONHAMPSTEAD. After 5 miles, at Reedy, turn right which will take you into the attractive village of Dunsford.

Ignore the side turnings and follow signs for DREWSTEIGNTON. Some 2¹/₄ miles beyond Dunsford, at a crossroads, turn left to cross the river Teign by Clifford Bridge (ROAD TO JOIN FOOTPATH FOR FINGLE BRIDGE).

Once over the bridge, keep right, and after ³/₄ mile bear right at a fork for CHAGFORD. At a T-junction turn right for CHAGFORD. At Easton, cross

Chagford is an ancient town, and was already important by the 12th century. In 1309 it was made one of the three (later four) Stannary Towns of Dartmoor, through which the government controlled the tin industry. This early importance and wealth had begun to fade by 1600.

Whilst it remained an important centre for markets and fairs, Chagford's streets and buildings reflect that decline – they have changed relatively little since the 17th century, which is of course what makes it a fascinating place. Some of the shops also seem to pride themselves on a policy of resisting change, and that again is part of Chagford's distinctive character.

the 'modern' A382, one of the few English A roads to have single track sections. Enter the small town of Chagford, and proceed to the square at its centre. If you don't already know Chagford, you should certainly park and explore it, but if you are not stopping, turn right at the top of the square, and pass the Bullers Arms pub.

Ogilby described the Exeter-Tavistock route as: 'affording an indifferent good road to Chagford, though hilly, but after over Dartmoor to Tavistock exceeding bad, being hilly, boggy and stony, without any accommodation.'

Today no sane walker on Dartmoor sets out without an Ordnance Survey map and a compass, but few if any 17th century travellers would have had a compass, and the best map available was Ogilby's own (see overleaf) which does not inspire confidence. For much of the way, there would have been no recognisable track, except where previous travellers had converged at a ford or a clapper bridge. It was extremely easy for travellers to get lost, especially if they were surprised by fog or snow.

There were no inns and very few habitations in which to take refuge. In other words, crossing the moor was a risky adventure, especially in winter. Strangers were better advised to go round the moor rather than over it.

Ogilby's map of the route across Dartmoor. All his maps were made in strip form, and presented as though they were scrolls

18

Part of Ogilby's Dartmoor crossing is now only possible on foot, but we shall follow the first few miles, then divert and join the turnpike road, which soon rejoins the ancient line.

Having turned right at the top of the square in Chagford, and passed the Bullers Arms, keep left down Manor Road (FERNWORTHY RESERVOIR). After 3/4 mile, bear left at a junction (FERNWORTHY RESERVOIR) then at the next junction bear left for POSTBRIDGE. (Ogilby's route went straight on here, but soon becomes a footpath – the Two Moors Way, Western Route.) Take the second on the right (JURSTON), keeping right at Jurston. This narrow lane eventually emerges onto the B3212, where you turn right.

The difficult section of the drive is over, and you can settle down to enjoy the beauty of the moor. Pass the Warren House Inn, which is where we rejoin Ogilby. Postbridge, a mile or so beyond this, is named from the 'post-road' which we are following, and is famous for its clapper bridge, a massive structure which has nevertheless been washed away from time to time by floods, but rebuilt.

At Two Bridges, we turn right, then keep right on B3357 TAVISTOCK. After a few miles, you will come to a high point where a very popular large car park on the left allows people to look at the extensive view westward. Descend for a mile. Just beyond Higher Longford, there is a crossroads, with a right turn to PETER TAVY and a left turn for WHITCHURCH DOWN/MOORTOWN. This was once the main Plymouth-Okehampton road, and, because both the A38 route and the Dartmoor crossing were impassable for wheeled traffic, an Italian prince who unwisely landed with his own coach at Plymouth in 1669 found he had to travel this way and via Okehampton and Crediton to get to Exeter!

If you don't already know Tavistock, then you should certainly go there and explore it, as it's a most inviting and interesting town, then return to this crossroads.

Otherwise, take the turn to WHITCHURCH DOWN, then follow signs to HORRABRIDGE. Descend into the village, turn left across the river bridge and continue up to the A386. Turn left here, and follow it to Yelverton. Turn left at the roundabout and take the B3212 up to PRINCETOWN. This is an old road, noted as a side turning on Ogilby's map, but in his day there was no settlement at Princetown. Continue beyond Princetown to Two Bridges, turn right and then left (B3212 MORETONHAMPSTEAD), retracing your route, but this time continue into and through Moretonhampstead towards DUNSFORD and Exeter (noting the almshouses on your left as you leave the town). This turnpike road has to go through some extraordinary contortions on its way down to Doccombe, and it is obvious from a map that there was an earlier route which was much more direct – but at the expense of gradients impassable for vehicles.

There is some beautiful wooded countryside on your way back past Steps Bridge. Just follow the signs for Exeter.

5 Exeter via Tiverton to Dulverton

Distance: 30 miles
Approximate time: 2 hours
Character: Beautiful countryside throughout. One narrow section between Silverton and Tiverton, but mostly quite reasonable country lanes.

From the Exe Bridges, follow the signs for CITY CENTRE and INNER BYPASS, climb the hill (crossing the line of the Roman city wall, with a pedestrian bridge over the main road) and at the traffic lights follow INNER BYPASS. At the first roundabout take the third exit (PINHOE/BROADCLYST) then at the next roundabout take the second exit, Old Tiverton Road.

After 1/2 mile, at a mini-roundabout, go forward (second exit) and immediately keep right, which is Stoke Hill. The road climbs, then descends steeply to a stream and climbs even more steeply up the other side, soon becoming a country lane of the kind which Ogilby-roaders will immediately recognise.

At Stoke Post keep left for STOKE CANON (the turning to POLTIMORE/ KILLERTON was the highway from Exeter to Taunton and Bristol) and fol-low the hill down to join A396. Cross the long medieval bridge across the River Culm and pass through Stoke Canon and then Rewe.

Some 0.8 miles after Rewe church, when the main road bears sharp left, carry straight on up a narrow lane, unsigned. Follow the major lane, which will bring you to Silverton, a particularly pleasant village – it used to be considered a borough town. After passing the Three Tuns turn right, to the central crossroads. It's worth stopping to take a closer look at the village.

Route A (authentic)

From the crossroads, turn left up Fore Street. The road climbs 600 ft. Pass Aishe Barton, a most attractive complex of buildings. Follow signs for BUT-TERLEIGH. Descend towards Butterleigh, then climb, but ignore the right turn to the church and pub and continue towards TIVERTON. The lane descends a steep hill, joins another road and continues down to a mini-roundabout, where you turn right, then descend further to a junction with A396. Turn left, then at the roundabout turn right into the town centre.

Route B (better)

From the crossroads, take 'Tiverton Road', out to the A396. Turn right. At Bickleigh, cross the river and keep right, into the outskirts of Tiverton. At the first roundabout turn right to cross the river. Forward at the second roundabout. At the third turn left, rejoining route A, into the town centre.

☞ You will pass on your left Old Blundells School, then cross the River Loman, which joins the Exe just below the town. This is apparently the origin of the name Tiverton, in Saxon *Twyfyrde*, or twin fords. After crossing the bridge, bear left up the main street, which soon becomes a one-way system, taking a compulsory right turn into Bampton Street.

At a junction controlled by traffic lights continue straight ahead. Pass the cemetery and head out of town. Turn right at a T-junction in a new

Tiverton is an ancient town (though devastated by major fires in the 17th and 18th centuries so there is little from the medieval period) with a castle, the old site of Blundells School, and a number of other interesting buildings – certainly a place to stop and explore.

In John Ogilby's time it was the most significant industrial town in Devon, producing huge quantities of woollen cloth. At that time, East Devon was a major producer of cloth, and was not finally outstripped by Yorkshire until the advent of steam powered looms in the mid 18th century.

estate, then first left (CHETTISCOMBE/CHEVITHORNE). Cross the A361 by a bridge, then immediately turn right (CHETTISCOMBE). Ignore the turning to Chevithorne, and pass on your left the woodlands of Knightshayes Court (National Trust).

The road now continues pleasantly and uneventfully for 5 1/2 miles, where it descends into the small market town of Bampton – though perhaps it should be described as a fair town, since its two fairs were among the largest in the south-west, and were a major outlet for livestock (cattle, sheep and ponies) from Exmoor.

At a T-junction, turn right, then shortly left (B3190 MOREBATH). Follow signs to MOREBATH. Within Morebath, turn left (MOREBATH CHURCH), then after 200 yards bear right. After less than mile you will arrive at a T-junction – except that it used to be a cross-roads. The track straight ahead was Ogilby's route: it heads steeply up the hill and even more steeply down into Bury. We have to make a detour, turning left and after a mile arriving at the A396, where we turn right, then after 500 yards turn right again, signed BURY. The road turns sharp left, rejoining Ogilby's track. At the next junction, continue straight ahead on the minor road into Bury.

This delightful village, a few hundred yards inside Somerset, was once a nodal point on the ancient road system. There is a packhorse bridge, which is presumably later than 1675, since Ogilby tells us the bridge was then made of wood, and a ford. After crossing the ford, we turn left and return to the main road, the lane to the right being a dead end.

Ogilby's route carried straight on here, climbing up a path which is now private, directly up that all but vertical hillside ahead, on its way to Minehead. You can, if you want, follow the Ogilby route by taking the road signed BROMPTON REGIS, then keeping left rather than going into Brompton, and following a lonely lane almost due north, to Timberscombe – after which the ancient track across the wooded hills to Minehead is now just a bridleway.

From Bury, we take the lane around the foot of the hill, turn left, then immediately right onto A396, and after 100 yards turn left for DULVERTON. This attractive town is very popular with visitors as a jumping off point for Exmoor, and is the home of the Exmoor National Park Authority.

6 Dulverton to Barnstaple

Distance: 26 miles
Approximate time: 1¹/4 hours
Character: For Ogilby, this was part of a much longer post-road, from London to Barnstaple, which made its way cross-country from Stonehenge to Bridgwater and then across the southern edge of the Brendon Hills and Exmoor to Dulverton. This section of it makes a pleasant drive.

From the town centre you have an immediate choice for the first half mile.

Route A (authentic)

Cross the bridge and immediately turn right, unsigned. After 150 yards, the road turns sharp left up a steep and narrow hill. After half a mile, turn right. (The road coming from the left here is the alternative, improved, route.)

Route B (better)

From the bridge, follow B3222 for 350 yards, then turn right (OLDWAYS END). This becomes a steep hill, but it is wider than Route A, which soon joins in from the right.

☞ Continue following signs to OLDWAYS END, turning right at a T-junction, then after about a mile keeping right into the village itself. Continue ahead, joining a slightly wider road and immediately leaving it (signed BOTTREAUX MILL).

Continue for 3³/4 miles along this ancient ridgeway – its age suggested by a prehistoric burial mound which lies alongside it but is not visible from the road. Ancient trackways frequently pass such 'barrows', though it is not always clear whether the barrow was constructed beside the track, or whether the earliest travellers used existing barrows as landmarks. Then join the B3227, which is the Bampton-Barnstaple turnpike road, dating from 1834. On reaching the A361, follow signs to join it heading for BARNSTAPLE. (Purists with the OS map Explorer 127 might want to take the Ogilby route through West Combsland and Aller Hill.)

Before long, turn left at a roundabout for B3227 SOUTH MOLTON, a substantial old town with a number of Georgian houses. Fork right at the end of the main street, then turn left B3227 TORRINGTON. Descend a long but gentle hill, then turn right for HILL VILLAGE. Just after the Stag's Head pub, turn left for FILLEIGH, passing the grand Georgian house, Castle Hill.

From Filleigh church, follow the SWIMBRIDGE road for 2 miles as far as Kerscott, then bear left (DENNINGTON/HANNAFORD). Follow signs to Hannaford. Within Hannaford, keep right (LANDKEY). Cross Hunnacott Bridge – not named, but it's signed as 'weak'.

At a fork, bear left (BABLEIGH), join another lane and almost immediately keep right. At a cross-roads, turn right (LANDKEY TOWN) and cross Landkey Bridge, then turn left at the church (BARNSTAPLE). At another crossroads, turn right then immediately left – ignoring the BARNSTAPLE sign. This ancient approach to Barnstaple will lead you over the modern A39, and down into Newport, a suburb of Barnstaple.

Go forward at traffic lights, keep left at a junction, and the road will lead you to the Long Bridge.

7 Circular tour from Barnstaple to Ilfracombe

Distance: 35 miles
Approximate time: 2 hours
Character: Ogilby showed two post-roads going to the port of Ilfracombe in 1675. The first, from Barnstaple direct to Ilfracombe, is familiar to locals as 'the middle road'. It is the shortest route, single track in places but nevertheless very useful when the main route through Braunton is likely to be congested – which is frequently.

Ogilby's second route goes directly from Ilfracombe to Bideford, using a ferry across the estuaries of the Taw and Torridge to Appledore. The ferry survived for foot passengers into the early 20th century, but the advent of wheeled vehicles in the early 19th century effectively caused the route to be abandoned; travellers went via Barnstaple instead. For parts of this tour and of the next, therefore, we shall have to substitute other old roads.

Leave the Barnstaple inner ring-road by A39 LYNTON, but at the first traffic lights turn left, and almost immediately right up the main street of Pilton.

You may think that Pilton looks like an interesting suburb of Barnstaple (and wonder, as I do, why Pilton Street is not full of antique shops) but Pilton is actually even older than Barnstaple. It was one of Alfred the Great's four Devon *burhs* – fortified settlements designed as a defence against Viking raids. Presumably the high ground around the church was more defensible than the lower ground on which Barnstaple was built, but by AD1000 the upstarts across the river were eclipsing Pilton.

At the top of the street keep left, and follow the main route through the village and its continuation, Bradiford. Once out of the village, keep right at the next two forks to and through Prixford and Guineaford. Continue north towards ILFRACOMBE, passing Marwood to the left. A long straight road then leads directly towards Ilfracombe, crossing A3123 (left then right), then being joined for 100 yards by B3230, before continuing down to ILFRACOMBE TOWN CENTRE.

Leave Ilfracombe by the LEE road, which bears right off the A361 BARN-STAPLE, then turns right and after 100 yards left, up Slade Road. This takes a winding route up the hill and turns sharp left just before the junction down to Lincombe and Lee Bay (which is a beautiful cove, if you don't already know it, and well worth a detour – park opposite the old school and church buildings, and walk down to the cove).

Continue ahead for MORTEHOE/WOOLACOMBE on a single-track lane with passing places. At the end of this lane, turn right onto the Woolacombe road, B3343, but very shortly keep left off it, for GEORGEHAM & CROYDE.

Ilfracombe was of course a port in the 17th century, which was why the post-roads went there: sea communications were all important, and the Post Office was a branch of the government, primarily concerned with carrying the King's (i.e. the government's) communications. The harbour area is of interest, but for the most part it is Ilfracombe's early days as a fairly genteel resort which define its architecture.

This road soon turns sharply right at a junction. After 400 yards, a bridle-way leading off to the left opposite cottages shows what Ogilby's roads must have looked like 350 years ago; it is very little changed and appropriately churned up by horses. If you have an OS map, you can see how it takes a short cut to Oxford Cross on its way towards Georgeham.

We continue cautiously to Georgeham, especially in the holiday season, when this narrow road is always busy. Georgeham was home to Henry Williamson, famous as the author of *Tarka the Otter*, though he would have preferred to be remembered for his many other novels.

At Forda, about 3/4 mile after Georgeham church, the lane towards Croyde takes a sharp right, where Ogilby's route went straight on, but that involves a bridleway. The older parts of Croyde are highly picturesque, and it manages to survive the crowds of surfers and family holidaymakers who descend on it every summer.

When the road forks near the post office, keep left. You will climb as you round the point, and suddenly the magnificent sight of Saunton Sands lies ahead of you, with Northam sands beyond, across the double estuary of the Taw and the Torridge – more than five miles where broad beaches meet the sea. The effects of waves and weather here can be highly dramatic.

Just over half a mile after you pass Saunton Sands Hotel, a bridleway emerging from the left is the Ogilby road; he has saved a couple of miles compared to our route. He then headed through the dunes on what is now the South West Coast Path. We must continue for just short of a mile, then turn right, BRAUNTON BURROWS, heading south.

Continue to the car park, for a short walk perhaps, then start to retrace your route, but turn first right along a lane (unsigned). This skirts the southern edge of Braunton Great Field, said to be one of only three fields in England still cultivated on the medieval strip system. In the early 20th century, 85 different farmers rented strips, but this is now down to a mere half dozen. At the end of this lane take the first left at the roundabout, then turn immediately right and follow South Street to the centre of this large village.

A short diversion reveals the old part, unseen from the main roads: turn left onto A361 in the Ilfracombe direction, then immediately turn right at the traffic lights. Bear left down Church Street (a 20 mph zone) and keep left at the church. At the T-junction turn left and return to the traffic lights.

Go forward at the lights, then take the first left (Heanton Street). Turn left at a junction, then first right along Lower Park Road. This becomes the Old Barnstaple Road, single track but with adequate passing places. Continue forward at two junctions, then join the lane from Prixford by which you left Pilton, and head back to the town centre.

To get to the start of the next tour, turn left at the bottom of Pilton Street, then right at the traffic lights. Turn right onto the inner ring road, round to the Long Bridge.

8   Circular tour: from Barnstaple to Bideford, Appledore and Torrington

Distance: 32 miles
Approximate time: 1 1/2 hours
Character: Pleasant countryside with three interesting historic towns, and a large coastal village with a famous, but threatened, shipyard.

If you have followed the previous circular tour to Ilfracombe, you will know that before the days of wheeled vehicles the ancient highway used a long-defunct pedestrian ferry from Saunton Sands to Appledore on its way to Bideford. Fortunately there is a pleasant road from Barnstaple to Bideford which was there in Ogilby's time – he indicated it as a side turning 'to Bediford' but did not map it in detail.

Leave Barnstaple by the Long Bridge and follow signs (A39) BIDEFORD. This involves a couple of mini-roundabouts, then a left turn at the next roundabout onto A3215. At the roundabout after this, turn right along Old Bideford Road, signed to HOLMACOTT and EASTLEIGH – both of them on your route.

New housing dominates the first section: proceed through a series of speed-reducing chicanes. When the suburban road curves to the right, turn left for HOLMACOTT and EASTLEIGH.

Now follow the major (well, the least minor!) road at all junctions. After

Bideford is an old town of much character, placed on a steep hillside, and its old main street (Mill Street) is pedestrianised. The town needs to be explored on foot rather than in a car, and there is plenty to see even if you don't fancy climbing the hill.

2¹/₂ miles you will pass under the A39, after which you follow signs to BIDEFORD. On the outskirts of Bideford you will reach a T-junction with a relatively new ring-road. (Old Barnstaple Road went straight on, but there is now no access.) Turn right at the T-junction, then left at the next T-junction (A386) which will take you into East-the-Water.

You now have the option of a tour to Appledore, returning to this spot, or you can head straight for Torrington, in which case turn left at the roundabout at the East-the-Water end of the bridge. Skip the next section.

To visit Bideford, Northam and Appledore

Turn right over the bridge, then right again along the quay. Follow the main road round a series of curves and up to a roundabout. Take the second exit and after half a mile ignore the major turning to the right (APPLE-DORE) but take the next turning right (TOWN CENTRE/NORTHAM BURROWS) which goes to the centre of Northam.

Opposite the church keep right and immediately right again (Diddywell Road). When the road narrows, turn left (Highbury Hill) and at the end of this road turn right, then immediately keep left into Long Lane. Ignore side turnings, and this will take you around the promontory and then along Appledore's quay. You will probably want to explore on foot the complex of narrow lanes. At the end of the quay, the main road turns inland and you have three choices.

You may prefer to take the first left, which will take you past the ship-yard – a splendid, if threatened, survival.

Alternatively take the second on the left, Pitt Hill. This is almost certainly the old highway, a classic Ogilby route, very steep and very narrow! Turn right at a T-junction.

Either way, you will need to turn left onto the main road, A386, and return to Bideford Long Bridge.

Or you could take the easiest route, the main road signed BIDEFORD.

☞ From East-the-Water to Torrington

Coming over the bridge, head straight ahead up the hill and follow the road past the former station. Continue up a long hill, then turn right at a mini-roundabout. Ignore the left turn and continue up Gammaton Road, once more climbing steadily. When the road curves left and downhill, take the country lane to the right – originally it would have been straight on – signed GAMMATON.

Since the bridge you have been following Ogilby's route: at last it begins to feel like it! After 1¹/2 miles, at a cross roads turn right (TORRINGTON). Keep left (TORRINGTON). Ignore side turnings. You will descend a steep hill to Huntshaw Mill Bridge: ignore turnings to either side and continue past Norwood Bridge to a junction with slightly wider roads. Turn right, then immediately left, which will take you up into Great Torrington, with the church directly ahead of you. The church may look medieval: in fact it replaced one which was blown up in 1645, during the Civil War.

If you don't intend to explore Torrington on this occasion, turn left and follow either Route A or Route B.

To explore the town on foot, turn right, then first left and left again to a large car park. (The Mole and Haggis bookshop carries a particularly wide range of Devon-interest titles.) After your exploration, turn left out of the car park, follow the street round to the right, and turn right at the T-junction onto the main road. You now have a choice of routes.

Route A (authentic but very narrow)

Take the second left, 50 yards before a roundabout, which is Gas Lane. Keep right. Gas Lane makes a steep and narrow descent, crosses a stream and climbs more gently up the other side of the valley. A slightly wider lane joins it from the left but we go straight on. We are heading for ALVERDIS-COTT, and we follow the major lane all the way.

At Alverdiscott we join the B3232, which is the modern Torrington to Barnstaple road – one which has attracted wry comments over the years, since it is as slow and winding as any inter-town route in the West Country. Whatever your usual opinions on the qualities of the B3232, after driving Ogilby's route you will think it motorway standard! It will take you to the outskirts of Barnstaple, at Roundswell, near the Sainsbury's superstore.

Route B

Continue to the roundabout and follow signs for B3232 BARNSTAPLE, which will take you to the outskirts of Barnstaple, at Roundswell, near the Sainsbury's superstore.

9 Barnstaple to Exeter

Distance: 42 miles

Approximate driving time: 2 hours

Character: The modern A377 is a slow road which winds gracefully along the Taw valley. Our ancient roads rarely wasted mileage winding about like that, but took the direct route. They never used river valleys because that requires engineering investment and reliable road maintenance. So Ogilby's route takes a much shorter line – but don't expect it to be quicker! This is deepest Devon with a vengeance, delightful but not to be hurried.

Starting from the Long Bridge on the town side, take the NEWPORT exit at the roundabout and follow the riverbank south, then turn right – it's unsigned except for speed humps! Cross Hollowtree Road at traffic lights.

Cross the A39 by a flyover, and immediately turn sharp right into Deer Park Road, at first parallel to the A39, then turning away. Keep left (VENN). Briefly join a lorry route and pass the Venn quarries. Descend into Bableigh, where you keep left uphill (COBBATON).

Ignore side turnings and follow signs to COBBATON. You will join a slightly wider lane. About 1 1/4 miles after this, you will pass a cottage called The Old Traveller's Rest – which Ogilby marked on his map as a wayside inn.

From Cobbaton follow signs for Chittlehampton. This is an attractive large village with a substantial church, St Hieritha, famous both for its unusual dedication and its magnificent tower. You will arrive at one end of the village street. Ogilby's route actually continued straight across here (CHITTLEHAMHOLT/SOUTH MOLTON) but I suggest you turn left (signed FILLEIGH) to stop and take a look at the village, and then return to this point to take the CHITTLEHAMHOLT road. Cross the B3227.

After 3 miles, pass through Chittlehamholt. At the foot of a long hill, join B3226. After 3/4 mile cross the River Mole and immediately turn left (KING'S NYMPTON), then shortly sharp right and steeply uphill (HILL HEAD/ SPITTLE). Follow signs to CHULMLEIGH.

Chulmleigh is a small town with a wonderful sense of belonging to a past and calmer age, set in beautiful countryside but unknown to almost all visitors to the county – indeed, probably to most Devonians as well! Head for the town centre and join B3096 for Chawleigh.

About 1 1/4 miles from the Royal Oak in Chawleigh, turn right at a minor crossroads (LAPFORD) and after 1 1/2 miles bear left, to pass through EAST-INGTON on your way to MORCHARD BISHOP.

Head south past the London Inn and after a further 1/3 mile keep left and follow signs for NEWBUILDINGS – one of those places that has never acquired a real name in hundreds of years, but remains for ever 'new' despite its very obvious and appealing antiquity.

Keep left here and follow signs to CREDITON. Turn right into a slightly wider lane from Sandford. At the point where you see the Crediton town sign, a few yards beyond a crossroads, bear right down Deep Lane. The ancient roads have often acquired the names Deep Lane or Dark or Darkey Lane, because relatively heavy use formed ever deeper 'holloways'.

Turn left at the T-junction then take the first right (Church Street).

Emerging onto the main road beside the church, turn left and follow A377 through Newton St Cyres to Exeter.

The post-road as shown by Ogilby crossed the river at Cowley Bridge, took what is now Cowley Bridge Road to the roundabouts in front of St Davids station, and then climbed St David's Hill to reach the city centre by North Street – an approach to the city which may well have remained unchanged since Roman times.

Crediton (or Kirton as it used to be known) was the site of a bishopric from 909 to 1050 when it was moved to Exeter. Crediton was given this honour not because of the size and significance of the town, as Exeter had been a major city since Roman times, but because it was the birth-place of St Boniface in 680.

---

10 A circuit from Exeter to Okehampton

Distance: 45 miles

Time: 1 1/2 hours

Character: A very easy route for both driver and navigator – by the standards of this book!

Since Saxon times if not earlier, there have been two possible routes from Exeter to Okehampton. One ran close to the northern edge of Dartmoor – approximately the route of the A30: in pre-turnpike times, the road surfaces between Exeter and Crockernwell were appalling even by prevailing standards, with slippery clay and loose stones, and there were serious hills at South Zeal and Sticklepath. The other route, via Crediton and Bow, then curving back south to Okehampton, was usually recommended to travellers as easier and less hilly but it could become impassable after heavy rain. Perhaps this is why neither of them was a post-road, as a result of which Ogilby did not map them.

We shall take the northern route on the outward journey, and return by 'the old A30' – though we shall always take the oldest available version of the road, so you may find some surprises.

Start by taking the A377 to Crediton, and follow it past Crediton's massive church with its unusual central tower – perhaps its medieval builders still yearned for its former cathedral status. Follow A377 for a further 2 1/4 miles beyond the church. Turn left for COLEFORD onto what is now a minor road (it used to be the main highway) and go forward at the crossroads in this attractive village, with its thatched cottages and inviting pub.

The 'Nymet' names in this area derive from an important sacred grove (*nemeton*) of the ancient Britons, and there was a Roman road here which ran through *Nemetostatio* (literally 'Grove Station') on its way west into Cornwall. The road ran parallel to the railway line and just a couple of hundred yards south of it, and a Roman fort – presumably *Nemetostatio* – is marked on the Ordnance Survey maps beside the river crossing.

Sticklepath

The word 'stickle' meant steep or difficult, and the path that gave the place its name still exists as a bridleway, which descends precipitously into the west end of the village. You might want to stop and take a look at it, and if you need a break, you might try the Devonshire Inn, a pub which retains (at the time of writing) its old character.

Continue in the same direction to Bow. Turn left onto the A3072 and pass through the village, which grew up along the highway in the 13th century. The original centre of the settlement lay to the south, near the parish church at Nymet Tracey.

Watch out for the splendid Elizabethan manor-house on your right, cross the river and keep left on B3215 for OKEHAMPTON. As so often happens, the original route into the town is blocked for traffic reasons, so we are directed to the left and arrive at a T-junction with B3260. To explore the town, turn right. To continue with the tour, turn left.

The A30 is now a dual carriageway all the way through Devon but the old turnpike road and, in places, its predecessors still exist. When you reach the dual carriageway, continue across and into Sticklepath.

At the far end of the village, cross the river bridge and immediately turn left – to the left of a thatched cottage. (The turnpike which goes straight on demonstrates superbly the skill of the early 19th century engineers in minimising the gradients, but we are following the older road so we turn left!) We climb, then descend into South Zeal.

South Zeal is a medieval planned town which never quite made it. Like Bow, it was carefully planned and deliberately sited on the highway away from its parish centre (South Tawton, half a mile to the north and well worth a diversion). Each property had a house on the street, and a long thin plot of land at the rear, a furlong deep.

In the 19th century, the nearby Ramsley Mine became very productive, so South Zeal was briefly a mining village. Many of the houses are medieval in origin, including the Oxenham Arms.

At the foot of the hill the village street bears left, then climbs steeply. Ignore the left turn, then keep left at the fork. This lane will in due course return you onto the turnpike. After one mile further, a house on the right is named Harepath. The Anglo-Saxon word for a main highway was *haerepath*, 'army road', so this truly is an ancient route. (There is another property also called Harepath just 2^1/$_2$ miles further east.) Continue to Whiddon Down, taking the first exit at the mini-roundabout, then crossing the A30 at a further roundabout, signed CROCKERNWELL.

At Crockernwell, notice how we pass the backs of cottages that were built to face an older and narrower line of the road.

At Cheriton Cross a flyover carries us over the A30 yet again, and into Tedburn St Mary. At the end of the village, we fork left (WHITESTONE), and continue through Whitestone and Nadderwater into the outskirts of Exeter. Ignore side turnings, take the second exit at a roundabout, at the bottom of a steep descent go forward at traffic lights, and before long you will arrive at the Exe Bridges by way of Okehampton Street.

11   Okehampton, Launceston and Hatherleigh

Distance: 54 miles

Time: 2^1/$_4$ hours

Character: Only a small part of this route (from Launceston to Halwill Junction) was mapped by Ogilby. The rest of the route is shown in Donn's map of Devonshire in 1765, and is almost certainly much older than that. It passes through pleasant countryside, little known to most visitors.

By 1765, the road from Okehampton to Launceston by way of Bridestowe and Lifton, later named the A30, had already been established as a turnpike. A map of 1695, however, which was probably based on Ogilby's own unpublished surveys, shows a different route, running to the north of Bridestowe, Thrushelton and Stowford, of which a few fragments are perhaps visible on a map (notably as a lane past Way Barton Farm and further west as a bridleway past Dingles Steam Village) but the Lewdown route was so superior that the ancient road has effectively disappeared and cannot now be followed even on foot.

So, instead of following 'the old A30' which is pleasant but a bit tame, I have preferred another old road, which takes us through the pretty village of Bratton Clovelly, and has all the character we expect from the ancient roads.

Starting from the traffic lights at the centre of Okehampton, take the road beside the White Hart Hotel which leads towards the station, then take the second on the right, Castle Road. This shimmies to the right to cross the West Okement River, then gives us a splendid view of the romantic ruins of Okehampton Castle, before joining New Road. After 400 yards, bear right and then at two mini roundabouts follow signs for HALWILL A3079. After a further 3¹/₂ miles, turn left (BOASLEY/BRATTON CLOVELLY).

Entering Bratton Clovelly, you may want to visit the church, which has a particularly fine interior with the remains of wall paintings; if not, then turn right, and after 100 yards, opposite the Clovelly Inn, left for BROADWOODWIDGER. After 2 miles at a junction follow BROADWOODWIDGER.

After a further mile, reaching a wider road, turn left (where a right turn would take you to Roadford Lake, with its lakeside walks and tearooms) and descend a gentle hill. From this point the construction of the modern A30 dual carriageway has totally disrupted the line of the old roads. The one you have been following carried straight on at the foot of the hill (KELLACOTT) then climbed; it can be seen passing close to the left of the beautiful clump of trees on the hilltop ahead of you and heads for Liftondown. That is no longer a through route.

So at the bottom of the gentle hill, noticing the village of Broadwoodwidger perching on a hill to the right, follow the road round to the left and cross the A30, then continue up to a crossroads. Turn right for LIFTON.

You can now either follow the obvious road (the former A30) through Lifton, or take a diversion onto the pre-turnpike line of the road: 300 yards after a factory on the left, on the apex of a bend, turn right into Old Tinhay. At a junction keep left; pass the school, then take the first right into Darkey Lane. There are a number of Dark, Darky and Darkey Lanes in Devon, as well as some Deep Lanes, and many are identifiably ancient roads: they were used more than other lanes so they became worn down as holloways, sometimes yards below ground level, shady and often deep in mud.

Launceston was once the capital of Cornwall, and there is a Norman castle as well as remnants of a town wall with a remarkable gateway, a church of carved granite, a surprising street of rather grand Georgian houses, and many nooks and quiet corners to explore on foot, not to mention a variety of small shops.

At the end of Darkey Lane, turn right (LAUNCESTON) to rejoin the main road. Cross under the A30 into Liftondown then continue down to Polson Bridge over the Tamar into Cornwall. You now have a choice: you can either explore Launceston – which gets relatively few visitors, though it is a fascinating hilltop town which people would rush to explore if it was in Tuscany – or you can by-pass it.

To explore Launceston, follow the signs up to the town, and find a car park. When you leave, follow signs for HOLSWORTHY A388, which will lead you down past the outside of the castle wall, to the suburb of Newport; turn right at a mini-roundabout and go forward at a second one. Once over the top of a hill and past a garden centre, you will spot a former toll-house on the right, where we rejoin the alternative route.

To avoid Launceston, take the first on the right after crossing Polson Bridge (ST LEONARDS) and follow the narrow lane uphill, keeping right at two forks, and emerging through Homeleigh Garden Centre (beware distracted shoppers); turn right onto A388 and pass the former Dutson toll-house.

☞ Descend to cross the Tamar. You get a good view of the late fifteenth century New Bridge on your right. Continue for two miles into St Giles-on-the-Heath, and turn right there onto a minor road for TOWER HILL and

Halwill station opened in 1879, and a few years later became a junction when the Bude line was opened. These lines into North Devon and North Cornwall were a folly on the part of the LSWR, as there was never the traffic to make them successful. They were axed in 1966 – a demise ironically remembered at Halwill Junction in the street name Beeching Close!

Hatherleigh is well worth a brief exploration on foot: it is a proud sur-
vivor from the days before our high streets became depressingly uni-
form, and is supported by an extensive rural community, coming fully
to life only on market day.

HALWILL. Ignore side turnings and head for HALWILL JUNCTION. Pass an
extensive forestry plantation on the right, ignore a left turn for STOWFORD,
then shortly at a cross roads turn left for HALWILL JUNCTION. Turn left onto
A3079.

Turn right at the mini-roundabout and follow signs for BLACK TOR-
RINGTON. After 3¹/₄ miles turn right onto A3072 HATHERLEIGH. Cross the
A386 at a roundabout, into Hatherleigh.

From the roundabout, keep left then turn right (MONKOKEHAMPTON).
In Monkokehampton, turn right onto B3217, the old Barnstaple to Okehampton road. Head south to Exbourne. Cross A3072 (BRIGHTLEY) and
continue south to enter Okehampton by way of an industrial estate.

We are obliged to turn left (ALL THROUGH TRAFFIC) rather than using
the old road, North Street, which lies straight ahead. Turn right at a mini-
roundabout, then right at a T-junction (TOWN CENTRE).

12 Tiverton Parkway to Exeter

Distance: 17 miles
Approximate time: 50 minutes
Character: The main road from Bristol to Exeter came through Wells,
Glastonbury, Middlezoy and Taunton to Wellington. Then it followed the
modern line of the A38 surprisingly closely to Waterloo Cross which is
about half a mile east of junction 27 on the M5. The second part of this
drive, from Cullompton to Exeter, goes through lovely country, and the large
village of Bradninch deserves to be better known.

From Junction 27, take the A38 WELLINGTON but after ¹/₂ mile turn sharp
right onto the B3181, which is the former A38, south to Willand. Go forward at a roundabout and after ¹/₂ mile turn left (POST OFFICE).

Keep right along a road called Willand Old Village. This soon rejoins the old main road. Cross the motorway and continue to Cullompton, keeping right at two mini-roundabouts and ignoring the left turn to the motorway junction. Follow B3181 through the town, but at a roundabout take the second exit for BRADNINCH.

Keep right within Bradninch on the SILVERTON road, then at a cross-roads go straight on for BROADCLYST/EXETER. After 1³/4 miles, join the B3185 near Silverton paper mills, keeping left to cross the River Culm. Fork right to pass across the entrance to Killerton House (National Trust). Ignore side turnings and climb steadily to a T-junction at Stoke Post.

Turn left here (EXETER 2) then keep right on the major road, which will lead you down a deep but wide holloway to Mincinglake Bridge – at which point you suddenly realise you are already in Exeter. Take the third exit at the roundabout to bring you to the top of Sidwell Street.

13 Axminster to Exeter

Distance: 24 miles
Approximate time: 1 hour
Character: This is part of Ogilby's main road into the South-West, the post-road from London to the Land's End. Its route is via Staines, Basingstoke, Andover, Salisbury, Shaftesbury, Sherborne, Yeovil and Crewkerne (that is, what would become the A30) but then diverting to Axminster.

From Axminster take the B3261 to join the A35 towards Honiton. At Kilmington, the old road took a more direct line, to the left of the war

Ogilby tells us that Bradninch 'before its devastation by fire enjoyed a market which is now disused'. Many Devon towns with their vulner-able cob and thatch houses experienced at least one devastating fire, but recovered: Bradninch continued to have wool and lace industries into the 18th century, and subsequently paper making at Hele, but its importance gradually dwindled.

memorial, but this is no longer a through route, so we follow A35 around the side of the hill. Some 2 miles after the Old Inn at Kilmington, turn right (DALWOOD/STOCKLAND), then immediately keep left. After 1¹/₂ miles, at a crossroads on a bend, turn left (WILMINGTON/HONITON) and descend steeply, crossing a railway line. Then turn right onto A35 for 2 miles, passing turnings to Offwell.

When you see a tower ahead of you, keep left (FARWAY/NORTHLEIGH) so as to pass just to the right of the tower. Go forward at a crossroads, and descend steeply towards Honiton, rejoining A35.

Pass through a pair of old turnpike gates, and keep left along Honiton's main street. Follow signs to join the A30 in the direction of Exeter, but take the first opportunity to leave it again, on B3177.

This is the Ottery road, and after crossing under the railway there is a left turn to Ottery. Don't take it, but carry straight on along the old main road through Fenny Bridges.

You need to turn left for FAIRMILE to avoid being funnelled back onto the A30. Reaching a T-junction, turn right (WHIMPLE) under the main road, then immediately left (WHIMPLE).

At a T-junction, turn right (WHIMPLE/ROCKBEARE) The road descends and bears gently left, opposite a small housing development. You have now rejoined the line of the Roman road heading direct for Exeter, passing just north of Rockbeare church, then of Clyst Honiton church.

At this point you may want to give up and follow the signs for Exeter and the M5.

If you want to be authentic, however, and don't mind going into Exeter, you should bear right 300 yards beyond the Duke of York pub at Clyst Honiton, onto Black Horse Lane. This was, I think, the line of the ancient highway, but it is now blocked by its successor the M5, so you need to turn right when you reach the blockage, then first left and keep left, over the motorway.

At a T-junction, turn left, then first right along Hollow Lane which despite development manages to retain something of the character as well as the name of an ancient road. On reaching the B3181, you will probably be obliged to turn left (the road was being redesigned when I last drove

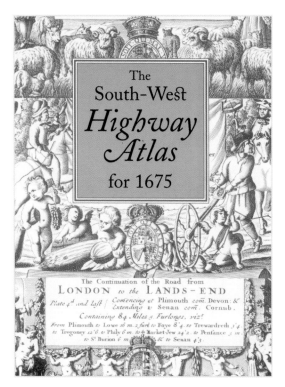

John Ogilby's own directions for the routes through Devon, and all his maps covering Devon, Cornwall, Dorset and Somerset, are to be found in The South-West Highway Atlas for 1675, *Paul White (Tamar Books, £9.99) which is available within the West Country from good bookshops or from the book distributor Tor Mark, (01209) 822101*

this way), but I think the old road probably went straight on here, through the hospital grounds to Whipton.

If you want a circuit, you could return to Axminster by Ogilby's Exeter-Lyme-Dorchester route – but as it scarcely seems to diverge from today's A3052, you won't need any special directions.

And so Godspeed you
but dont expect to average more than 15-20mph!